Fruit of the Spirit

"But the fruit of the Spirit is love, joy, peace, longsuffering, gentleness, goodness, faith."

Galatians 5: 22

Dear Reader —

Herein I have tried to mirror the rich philosophy of — the attitude of gratitude, the joy of sharing, the warmth of love, the music of laughter, and the power of faith. I sincerely hope this book will please you and strengthen your faith.

    Yours in Christian brotherhood
      Beatrice Branch
        1970

Fruit of the Spirit

by Beatrice Branch

Barry College Library
Miami, Florida

The Naylor Company
Book Publishers of the Southwest
San Antonio, Texas

Copyright ©, 1970 by BEATRICE BRANCH

This book or parts thereof may not be reproduced without written permission of the author except for customary privileges extended to the press and other reviewing agencies.

Library of Congress Catalog Card No. 77-127131

ALL RIGHTS RESERVED

Printed in the United States of America

SBN 8111-0365-X

This book is dedicated
TO MY MOTHER
whose faith has been a constant goad
AND MY HUSBAND
whose love gave inspiration

Acknowledgments

Gratefully this author acknowledges the kind permission of editors to include herein poems that have appeared in these publications: *Church Management, Denver Post Poetry Forum, Hearthstone, Home Life, Ideals, Mature Years, Prize Poems* (Greater Miami Poetry Festival), *Sunday Digest, The Christian, The Christian Home, The Christian Home Messenger, The Methodist Woman, The Reporter "Of Men And Dreams," The Youth's Instructor, Time Of Singing,* and *World Call.*

Acknowledgment is also made of quotations from the King James and Revised Standard Version of the *Bible*, and "Renascence" by Edna St. Vincent Millay.

Sincere gratitude is herewith extended to dedicated teachers and librarians who early revealed to me the beauty and wonder of words, to faithful ministers and Sunday school teachers who directed me to the significance of the Word, and to Vivian Laramore Rader, beloved Poet Laureate of the State of Florida, who stirred the latent embers of imagination and kindled the fagots of sensibility within.

Special thanks are due the friends in Laramore Rader Poetry Group and Riverside United Methodist Church, Miami, whose encouragement and helpfulness made this book a reality.

Special reprint permission to use copyrighted material was given as follows: David C. Cook Publishing Company for "Compassion," first published in *Sunday Digest*; The Methodist Publishing House for "Too Soon the Carols

Fade," "Strength," and "Waiting for Santa," first appearing in *Mature Years* and the latter reprinted in *The Reporter*; Sunday School Board of The Southern Baptist Convention for "Letter to a Serviceman" from *Home Life*.

Contents

Love and Joy

Golden Cocoon	3
Beauty	4
Hobbies	5
Country Doctor	6
Village Queen	7
Blood Bank	8
Basic Arithmetic	9
These Are My Gifts	10
Brothers	11
Ode To John Brown	12
In the Interest of Safety	13
No Richer Gift	14
Lamp of Friendliness	15
Christmas Eve	16
My Christmas Tree	17
Thanksgiving	18
Our Daily Bread	19

Peace
Peace Is Born of Love	23
Brotherhood	24
Hatred Is a Heavy Weight	25
Understanding	26
Knowledge	27
Gateway To Peace	28
Storms of Discontent	29
War	30
Too Soon the Carols Fade	31
Promise of Springtime	32
Easter Benediction	33

Longsuffering
Letter To a Serviceman	37
Waiting for Santa	38
Comfort	39
Auf Wiedersehen	40
Lonely Hearts	41
Shadows	42
Strength	43

Gentleness and Goodness
More Than a Dream	47
Man Now Desires the Moon	48
Dexterity	50

Compassion	51
The Color of Words	52
Modern Pharisee	53
Paths	54
Bittersweet	55
Fruits of Discipline	56
Wise Philosophy	57
Reflection	58
Temptation	59
Trapped	60
Judge Not	61
Contrition	62
Home Mission	63

Faith

"The Way of the Cross Leads Home"	67
Faith	68
Mother's Day	69
Laurels	70
Life's Measurement	71
There Are Many Who Doubt	72
Biography	73
Too Late	74
This Is My Song	75

Love and Joy

Love

"Better is a dinner of herbs where love is,
than a fatted ox and hatred with it."

Proverbs 15: 17

Joy

"Thou dost show me the path of life;
in Thy presence there is fullness of joy,
in Thy right hand are pleasures for evermore."

Psalms 16: 11

Golden Cocoon

There are folk
Who bear the yoke
Of stubborn prejudice.

Some there be
Who shamelessly
Are ruled by avarice.

Yet many find
True peace of mind
In love's warm chrysalis.

Beauty

"Mirror, mirror on the wall,
Who is fairest of them all?"
Quickly Wisdom's voice replies,
"Love is fairest. Loving eyes
See in each familiar face
Inherent loveliness and grace."

Hobbies

Collectors rummage near and far
For items in particular;
And hobbyists pursue with zeal
The avocations that appeal;
But life's most fruitful dividends
Are paid to those collecting friends.

Country Doctor

He quickly goes where anyone
Suffers pain. In heat of sun
Or starlit icy cold, his code
Takes him afar to lift the load
Of suffering. He senses grief,
If naught but passing brings relief;
Delight is equally sincere
When loving care brings health and cheer.

He has no bulging bank account,
But riches are not paramount
Within his dream. He has rewards
In friendly smiles and grateful words.
With deep concern for those distressed,
He gives to each his very best
And, following a higher plan,
Daily serves his fellowman.

Village Queen

Amanda could not read or write
    And Trouble knew her name,
But any trial that he brought
    Her laughter overcame.

She wore responsibility
    Like a jeweled crown,
Wrapping self within the folds
    Of Friendship's regal gown.

Throughout the village she was seen
    Wherever someone's need
Afforded opportunity
    To do a kindly deed.

Amanda never went to school
    Or won the world's acclaim,
Yet in the gallery of love
    She stands with those of fame.

Blood Bank

Here kindly donors can repay
The crimson wealth spent yesterday.
A pulsing heart and selfless mind
Render service, undefined,
To those to whom such riches give
Another chance to laugh and live.

Basic Arithmetic

Loving adds pleasure,
Labor and tears,
But pays in subtraction
Of lonelier years.

Multiplied quantities
Give life design —
And often, division
Can strengthen the vine.

These Are My Gifts

These humble gifts, Lord,
    I joyfully bring:
The myrrh of compassion
    To ease suffering,
The fragrance of blossoms
    To lessen despair,
And that golden treasure —
    The blessing of prayer.

I offer these gifts,
    In the name of the Lord,
To those who are lonely
    Or ill in a ward.
I have little to render
    Of earth's currency,
So I bring only love
    As my gift for Thee.

Brothers

Since every man is but a link
Dependent on the strength of others,
Why is it that some mortals shrink
From calling all of mankind brothers?

Ode To John Brown

Today your body is but molding dust
Beside a giant boulder on a hill,
But followers have fostered freedom's trust
And those who hold your hope remember still.
The ripened seeds of justice do not die;
Nurtured in some heart, they sprout and live
To blossom in the garden of advance.
Historians do not deny
(Though equity is yet diminutive)
You gauged young Liberty's significance.

In the Interest of Safety

Good Will
is a shovel that can help to clear away
the drifts of intolerance
now choking the paths of peace;
is the salt that can melt away
the sleet of misunderstanding
that prevents world travelers
from having a firm foothold on the road of love;
is the wiper that can sweep away
the rain of selfishness
obstructing the vision
of dangers and beauties that lie ahead;
is the lamp that can brighten the way.
Therefore, in the interest of our own safety
and that of others,
let us hold fast to
Good Will.

No Richer Gift

Within her veins there flows a blend
    Of varied ancestry,
Endowing an inherent charm
    That everyone can see.

Though work has traveled at her side
    From early childhood years,
Good humor and a ready smile
    Deny a cause for tears.

Unselfishness has always been
    Her life's philosophy;
She — with little, lends her strength
    Wherever want may be.

Her heart and hands she freely gives
    To anyone in need,
And who could grant a richer gift
    Or have a better creed?

Lamp of Friendliness

Meeting face to face,
She notes this aging one
Is not the beau ideal in dress or figure —
Yet some magnetic charm compels her scrutiny.
He gazes into twinkling eyes,
Discovering they are not springtime blue,
But still reflect the stars
And reawaken dreams too long forgotten.

Smiling, they voice a cheerful greeting,
And in this brief encounter
Are spirits warmed and hopes renewed.
Continuing their ways, each moves ahead
With a surer step and a lighter heart,
As the lamp of friendliness
Makes bright the path of yesterdays.

Christmas Eve

Tonight some magic sets my feet
Upon a starlit village street.
Trudging up the snowy road,
I sense a gaiety — bestowed
By that expectancy I knew
When youth and I kept rendezvous
With Christmastide. Candles, bright
Against the frosted pane, invite
Me home. The welcoming hello
Of loved ones brings a warming glow.
That special corner by the stair
Is livened by a spruce, made fair
With ropes of popcorn, candy canes,
Iced gingermen and paper chains.
Before the bedtime hour has rung,
Familiar carols have been sung
And Grandpa, once again, has told
Of the Messiah born of old.
Holding fast reality,
With gratefulness I turn the key
Within the lock that holds the past
To count the blessings there amassed.

My Christmas Tree

Since ornaments that grace my tree
Are gifts the years bestow on me,
Each Christmastide I find the store
Of trimmings greater than before.

Atop the tallest branch a bright
Haloed star illumes the night,
Holding fast within its glow
The many loves that helped me grow.

Winged angels on my evergreen
Are educators I have seen
Lifting high the torch of praise
To guide a youngster through the maze.

To this rich stock of jeweled cheer
Time is adding, year by year,
More ornaments of rainbow hue
Spun from blessings that accrue.

Thanksgiving

The golden treasures I possess,
The many blessings that are mine
Fill my heart with thankfulness.

Even sorrow's deep distress
Can only for a while outshine
The golden treasures I possess.

Some days are cloudy, I confess,
Yet rainbow tints in life's design
Fill my heart with thankfulness.

Never can I quite express —
Nor can I readily define
The golden treasures I possess;

But the warming glow of love's caress
And the rosiness of friendship's wine
Fill my heart with thankfulness.

Remembering when I had less,
My gratitude and joy combine.
The golden treasures I possess
Fill my heart with thankfulness.

Our Daily Bread

These four are creatures' basic needs:
Food, drink, rest and warmth.

However plain the fare may be,
All seek their food hungrily.

Drink quenches nature's thirst;
Without it, life would be accursed.

Each must rest a certain while,
In journeying along life's mile.

Were there no warmth, no light, the earth
Would hold no beauty, give no birth.

How blest am I that land and sea
And sky fulfill these needs for me.

Peace

"Peace I leave with you,
My peace I give unto you;
not as the world giveth, give I unto you.
Let not your heart be troubled,
neither let it be afraid."

John 14: 27

Peace Is Born of Love

Speak words of love
While you may,
Lest there befall
Your heart someday
The sad regret
You did not bare
The tenderness
Existent there.

Remember well:
Man's year is brief;
Remorse foments
An endless grief.
Speak words of love
To queen or king —
Then all your days
Your heart can sing.

Brotherhood

If there were perfect friendliness,
Each man might realize his dream.
How many nations peace might bless,
If there were perfect friendliness;
No heart would bow beneath distress,
No one would ever feel supreme.
If there were perfect friendliness,
Each man might realize his dream.

Hatred Is a Heavy Weight

Unloveliness is all around,
But those who love have vantage ground
From which the mortal faults they see
Are viewed with magnanimity.
God alone can understand
Why any wear a certain brand.

Antipathy can make one sad;
Affection blesses and makes glad
The hearts that earnestly enfold
The richness of its precious gold.
Life, at best, is much too brief
To burden hearts with hatred's grief.

Understanding

"Give me understanding and I shall keep Thy law; yea, I shall observe it with my whole heart." Psalms 119: 33

Intolerance is cold and sly;
Like autumn's hand on bending rye,
Its hoary fingers spread their mark
Over lands that soon are stark.

Understanding's warmth can melt
The ice, as drops of April pelt
Against the snow on bank and lea,
Returning it to a thirsty sea.

When violent winds no longer blow,
In mellow clay the embryo
Of seeds that slept a while, subdued,
Will root and rise to magnitude.

Knowledge

My spirit knows that anger is a test
For those who let emotion domineer;
An errant thought can rob the night of rest,
Can goad unpleasant dreams that persevere.

Disloyalty is like a glancing spear
That cuts into a friend's unarmored breast.
Despite the pain that follows every jeer,
My spirit knows that anger is a test.

The selfish way becomes the stoniest,
Though its signboard reads, "For peace, turn here."
Many obstacles are manifest
For those who let emotion domineer.

Sincerity creates an atmosphere
Of warmth, and ever is a welcome guest,
But wrath can make a sunny day seem drear;
An errant thought can rob the night of rest.

Who wants the crumbs of favor, second-best
To love's heart-warming jeweled cup of cheer?
Hungering for manna that is blest
Can goad unpleasant dreams that persevere.

How often anger whispers in my ear,
Insisting I obey his bold behest,
But just behind him is a lonely bier;
He wears a shroud beneath his scarlet vest —
          My spirit knows.

Gateway To Peace

In every hemisphere
Throughout this planet, Earth,
Countless tongues have prayed
That peace may have rebirth.

All seek a miracle
And ask that Wisdom stay
The clutching hand of fear
Hiding sunlight's ray.

Such a miracle
The Holy Word expounds:
Within true brotherhood
Lasting peace abounds.

The gate that leads to peace
Is arched with deep concern
For all of humankind
Making life's sojourn.

Storms of Discontent

Closer come the bolts of lightning,
   Threatening humanity.
      Frightened by war's claps of thunder,
      Fearfully men run and hide.

Winds of tension, wildly heightening,
   Drown love's joyous harmony,
      Tear man's hope of peace asunder,
      Strip the nations of their pride.

Long has man been groping blindly
   In the darkness of this storm;
      Long his soul has been denuded
      By the tempest of his mind.

Will he always think unkindly
   And his heart refuse to warm
      Toward the varied types included
      In this world that God designed?

War

Life is filled with fear.
Man has faced it in the fray
Since first he used a stony spear;
He finds it everywhere today.
Life is filled with fear.

War brings many hearts dismay,
Robs families of those held dear
Who have become an enemy's prey.
O, why does hatred persevere?
There must be a better way!

Too Soon the Carols Fade

Across the world the bloody stain
Of hatred creeps, making gain
As it has done since time began,
When right to choose was given man.

Each Christmastide a holy light
Attempts to stay this spreading blight.
For just a while, eyes will turn
Heavenward, and may discern
The meaning of this starry glow
And sense the warmth it can bestow.

But all too soon man's lowered eyes
Will seek the feeble alibis
For missile bases, rockets, walls,
And everything that disenthralls.

Promise of Springtime

Each Christmas we follow the star for a while
And find in our beings a glow and a smile.
Empowered by habit, our footsteps return
To pathways concreted with worldly concern.

With promise of springtime, thoughts turn aside
To ponder the magic of earth's Eastertide;
But soon we are weighted with burdens of flesh,
As tighter our senses are twisted in mesh.

Good Shepherd, take pity on sheep that have strayed
And wander in darkness, alone and afraid;
Come to the rescue. We covet release
From all that estranges the blessing of peace.

Easter Benediction

This Sacred House
Affirms the peace
That bids all doubt
And anger cease.

Above the soft,
Piped notes is heard
The witness of
A golden bird.

An empty cross
Is banked with white,
And streaming rays
Of rainbow light

On aisle and pew
Make very real
The One before
Whose throne we kneel.

Longsuffering
(Patience and Fortitude)

"I . . . beseech you to walk worthily
of the calling wherewith ye were called,
with all lowliness and meekness,
with longsuffering,
forbearing one another in love;
giving diligence to keep the unity of the Spirit
in the bond of peace."

Ephesians 4: 1-3

Letter To a Serviceman

I sing a song when skies are blue
And hum a tune when skies are grey,
Pretending I am there with you.

How long it is since our adieu!
Because you begged me to be gay,
I sing a song when skies are blue.

Whenever letters are too few,
I live again each yesterday,
Pretending I am there with you.

I think about the joys we knew —
And just to still my heart's dismay,
I sing a song when skies are blue.

I scan the papers for a clue
To how much longer you must stay —
Pretending I am there with you.

Your face is always in my view,
And though I don't forget to pray,
I sing a song when skies are blue,
Pretending I am there with you.

Waiting for Santa

"Oh, Christmas is for youngsters."
    We are very often told —
But isn't it for oldsters, too,
    For just how old is "old"?

The Santa of the elders' dreams
    Is no immortal elf
Who climbs down chimneys Christmas Eve
    To leave gifts on a shelf.

He can be almost anyone
    Who brings a bit of cheer,
Or offers some encouragement,
    Or wipes away a tear.

How sorrowful to watch and wait
    With eyes upon the clock,
Yet see no friendly, smiling face
    Or hear no welcome knock.

But years need not rob men of hope
    Or veil their dearest goals,
For all the joy of Christmas comes
    To men with love-filled souls.

Comfort

Beyond this form — sleeping, still,
I find a cross upon a hill.
My footsteps lead to a hallowed tomb,
Seeking there the Person whom
They crucified. The stone is rolled
Away; within, my eyes behold
An empty sepulcher. Dismayed,
Alone, my heart is sorely weighed
With sorrow; then the whirring wing
Of a gentle Dove gives comforting.

Auf Wiedersehen

We drain the dregs of parting's woe
As one by one we watch them go.
At first we sense a strange dismay;
Then, as hours are sped away,
Our hearts are comforted, as He
Has promised mournful hearts will be.

Long after fallen tears have dried,
Retrospection can provide
The joy that time has emphasized.
As yesterdays are well apprized
In quiet of a starry night,
Vision gains a deeper sight.

Lonely Hearts

The dues in this auxiliary
    Have always been too high,
Yet rolls of membership are great,
    Statistics verify.

At meetings some wear crinoline
    Beneath which grief can hide;
Some are gowned in somber black —
    All jauntiness defied;

Some are girded with a faith
    That gives their figures style;
But all discover loneliness
    Is lessened by a smile.

Shadows

When somber shadows hide the sun,
Many — blinded by the dark,
Helpless, stumble down the path
And fall into temptation's pit.
Some wander in a maze of woe,
Lose their way and are devoured
By gnashing jaws of bleak despair.
Many drown in sorrow's depth.
Some loop their ropes around the limbs
Of naked trees of memory
And strangle all tomorrow's joy.
Others check the steady flow
Of rich red blood of happiness
By wielding cynicism's blade.
But wisdom — cleansed by fallen dew,
Refreshed by evening quietude,
Watches darkness change to light,
Eager for the day ahead.

Strength

Like biblical Job,
Man suffers the pain
Of wounds in the flesh
And throes of the soul;
But burdens are lightened,
When faith is secure
That Christ knows full measure
Of all we endure.

Gentleness and Goodness

"Do all things without murmurings and disruptings;
that ye may be blameless and harmless,
children of God without blemish
in the midst of a crooked and perverse generation,
among whom ye are seen as lights in the world,
holding forth the word of life; . . ."
Philippians 2: 14-16

More Than a Dream

Life is more than complacency —
    More than a dream,
More than a song
    With a beautiful theme.

Life is weaving the seconds,
    The hours, the days
Into garments of usefulness
    Worthy of praise.

Man Now Desires the Moon

Today man walks in outer space,
Leaving footprints on the moon,
Abating her romantic grace.
Man has photographed her face
And wounded her with a harpoon.
It seems he won't be satisfied
Till her perimeter is strewn
With rubbish and her surface hewn.
While women watch with fearful pride,
"The world stands out on either side."

Who is man? that he should dare
To settle down upon her lap
And stroke his fingers through her hair,
Boldly hoping she will bare
The mysteries beneath her wrap.
He seeks her as an earthly bride —
For man has worn a wishing cap
As long as earth has had a map;
Yet he can make his cosmic stride
"No wider than the heart is wide."

If only man were not so blind
To all around him, he might see
That here are wounds he ought to bind
And here are needs of humankind
Within his own proximity;
But these he does not classify
As being the important key
To happiness. Wistfully
He elevates his yearnings high;
"Above the world is stretched the sky."

The race for power has begun.
No nation now will be content
Until all rivals are outdone
And all of outer space is won.
Man feels this is expedient —
Though woman often questions why.
Therefore, the scientists invent
Rockets for the steep ascent,
Acknowledging a heart can fly
"No higher than the soul is high."

Dexterity

A woman who has mastery of life
Crowds gentleness into her busy hours,
As she would tuck a bit of fernery
Into a bowl to accent vivid flowers.

Compassion

"Which of these three proved neighbor . . . ?"
Luke 10: 63

Three men, each with a different code,
Walk one by one along life's road.
The first one turns at the trail marked "Greed"
Without a thought for those in need.

The second plods with inward gaze,
Feeling no hate, giving no praise.
Indifference lights up the sign
That points to the pathway called "Just Mine".

The third man heeds the troubled cry
Of every stranger passing by.
He pauses at his brother's side
To bind his wounds or be his guide.

Three men traverse life's promanade —
Two walk alone — one walks with God.

The Color of Words

Cleverly some blend the hue
Of wisdom's humor with the true
Spectrum of adversity.
Many paint revengefully
In vivid tones of glaring red.
Across some canvas will be spread
The somber tones of suffering;
Some will mirror gentle spring.

Since deep emotion can direct
A brush in all it would project,
An artist has full mastery
Of brush and palette constantly —
For when these colors have been placed,
They never can be quite erased.

Modern Pharisee

Since Annie came to live with me
It seems that we cannot agree.
For instance: just a week ago,
That night we had the ten-inch snow,
A ragged tramp came to my door.
I had refused him twice before,
So quickly sent him on his way.
When he had gone, I heard her say,
"His hunger must be very great
For him to thus humiliate
Himself. How sad to be denied
Three times. I wish sincerely I'd
Been in your place and had the right
To ask him in to spend the night."
Poor Annabell could never save;
The little bit she had, she gave
Away — then had no place to stay.
Of course she helps me — but I pay
Her well; she has her board and room.
She thinks I'm wealthy, I presume;
Wants me to feed each wanderer.
Thank goodness, I am not like her!

Paths

When paths are straight
And vistas wide,
Man journeys on
With steady stride.
When forks appear,
No mortal may
See far ahead
In either way;
Yet one must choose
And never know
Where winding paths
He spurns might go.
His choice must here
Be very wise.
Beyond each fork
The future lies
For younger lads
Behind his back,
Who might pursue
His narrow track.

Bittersweet

Motor vehicles that man employs
Move eagerly along a street
Where children play — too young
To recognize
Harm's face.

Space
Assumes the guise
Of an imp, with honeyed tongue
Suggesting that the pace be fleet.
With power and excitement the decoys,
A speeding giant frequently destroys
The vigor of the indiscreet
And heady ones, who flung
Away life's prize
Apace.

Embrace
No more unwise
Use of power strung
Within the mighty, bittersweet
Motor vehicles that man employs.

Fruits of Discipline

"Train up a child in the way he should go . . ."
                                                Proverbs 22: 6

"Gee, Dad, why are you so cross
When accidentally I toss
A ball and break a window glass,
Or grumble over cutting grass?
Didn't you sometimes destroy
Or skip a chore, when just a boy?"

"Your father, Son, was much like you.
He did some mischief, that is true,
And many nights he sadly wept
Quite secretly before he slept.
He knows the problems of your years
And, if he sometimes interferes
Or scolds for something you have done,
It is because he wants his son
To have the privilege of mirth —
And yet appreciate the worth
Of understanding right and wrong.
A father's love is deep and strong;
He really isn't being cruel
When he resents a broken rule —
For love can truly be expressed
In many ways not manifest.
Youth, accepting discipline,
Will have a better chance to win
Full manliness — a prize to hold
More precious than a miser's gold."

Wise Philosophy

When a minister who did not cry
At leaving us was questioned why,
He offered us a golden key
To his very wise philosophy.

"If separations made my wife
And me lament, our changing life
Would just be spent in wiping tears
Away. As each new parting nears,
I am reminded none can know
What lies ahead — that each must go
Wherever duty's voice may call,
Not looking back regretting all
The joy he leaves, but looking up
With faith that God will fill his cup."

That gentle voice no more is heard,
For he is reaping life's reward;
But this bright key of jeweled gold
Is the symbol of a Christian's mold.

Reflection

Who sees another's weaknesses
    Reflected from his own,
Is less inclined to criticize
    Or throw a deadly stone.

Temptation

Some crave forbidden fruit;
Perhaps because it is denied,
Much time is spent in its pursuit.
In every land, nation-wide,
Some crave forbidden fruit.

Never satisfied,
Many become dissolute,
Forfeiting their manly pride
Because their souls are destitute,
Never satisfied.

Trapped

With cool
Bubbling laughter
And deep forgetfulness,
Bacchus beguiles the masses to
His trap.

The lock
Is then secured,
Determining the fate
Of those his empty promises
Betray.

Judge Not

*"He that is without sin among you,
let him first cast a stone at her."*
                              John 8: 7

O, why
Should gossiper
Condemn and crucify
The ones who bow their heads in shame —

The weak who love, not wisely but too well,
And thus create within their hearts a hell?

Is there among us one who does not err,
Who has the right to be a connoisseur

And cast a stone and sin disclaim —
Who has no need to pry
The log from her
Own eye?

Contrition

I can't atone
For wrongs that I did yesterday;
I can't atone
For oats that I have wildly sown.
I can't remold the potter's clay;
I simply can repent and pray;
I can't atone.

Home Mission

I cannot journey far across the earth
To minister and tell of Jesus' birth,
But with the mission voices I can blend
My own — in service here and gifts I send;
And if I have no strength or gifts to share,
I still can serve through witness, love, and prayer.

Faith

"Now faith is
the substance of things hoped for,
the evidence of things not seen."

Hebrews 11: 1

"The Way of the Cross Leads Home"

I often heard my mother sing
The hymns that told of Jesus' love.
Her hallelujahs now are sung
With Heaven's angel choir above.

Long ago my mother taught
My childish lips how to pray;
The Christian faith that she revealed
Sustains my aching heart today.

I kneel before an empty cross,
Reassured that there will be
A resurrection of the soul,
Through Jesus, for eternity.

Faith

I must hold fast to you.
Faith colors all I speak;
Refreshing as the dew,
Without you life is bleak.

Faith colors all I speak.
Your wisdom is profound;
Without you life is bleak;
In you all joys abound.

Your wisdom is profound,
Refreshing as the dew;
In you all joys abound;
I must hold fast to you.

Mother's Day

A year ago I picked a bloom
    Of crimson spiciness
And hummed a tune of gaiety
    As I pinned it on my dress.

Today my eyes reflect the dew
    On a fragrant snowy flower,
But faith accords the needed strength
    To face this lonely hour.

Laurels

She could not run or dance or swim
Since that disastrous ride with him,
When skidding wheels and crushing weight
Of metal cruelly changed her fate —
Confining her to bed or chair.
Despite her faith and fervent prayer,
There was small hope this interlude
Would end and strength would be renewed.

Resigned, she quested ways that she
Might help to serve humanity.
Her youthful intellect was wise;
Her hands were strong; her probing eyes
Were bright and clear. These three were still
The keys unlocking doors of skill.
With confidence she played life's game;
Now scientists revere her name.

Life's Measurement

No earthly instrument determines length
Of life or weight of character and strength,
For such dimensions (reason will apprise)
Hold magnitude beyond man's scope and size.

Upon this star there is no standard scale
For gauging mortal worth in full detail,
Yet life's capacity is well defined
In Christ, the perfect stature of mankind.

There Are Many Who Doubt

"Except I see ... I will not believe."
John 20: 24

A guiding star and virgin birth
    Were met with disbelief.
Lazarus, raised from the dead
    To assuage his sisters' grief,
Was not enough. Now devils flee;
    The lame can walk; the blind
Can see the light of day; and still
    The unbelievers find
Some scientific reason why
    Such miracles are wrought.
On Calvary they crucified
    The king the world had sought.
The darkened sky, the rending quake
    Were signs — that all might know
Jesus, perfect son of man,
    Had suffered every woe
For mankind's immortality.
    They overlooked each sign
(Though some were troubled by their fear)
    So proof He was divine
Was offered in the empty tomb.
    These miracles portray
To some that Christ was prophet, saint;
    He said, "I am the way . . .
And no man cometh . . . but by Me."
    The Scriptures can refute
Each doubter's argument, and God
    Is never destitute
Of proof for every claim therein;
    And yet, the Spirit Guide
Marks the way to eternity —
    Then lets each man decide.

Biography

A cry, a laugh,
a prayer, a groan —
then earth recalls
her mystic loan,
affixing life's
biography
to annals of
eternity.

Too Late

The scarlet bud, with petaled eyelids
closed against the scorching sun,
does not observe the trace of shadows
gathered on the lawn;
nor does the yellowed leaf,
clinging to the thorny stem
in one last vain attempt
to draw moisture from the fissured clay.
Neither sense the cooling breeze
that stirs the sullen air
high in the trees.
When unexpected rumbles shake the skies,
the languid rosebud only sighs —
aware this promise many times
is given carelessly.
Not until the pelting drops
have satisfied its doubt,
is faith restored within the bud —
but for a crumpled leaf
it is too late.

This Is My Song

My song has oftentimes been sung
In many lands, by old and young —
For every heart must hold some hope,
And most men fearfully will grope
For something to which they can cling,
When threatened with life's perishing.

My lyrics sing of faith and praise,
Of sunny skies and cloudy days;
The melody is thankfulness
For blessings that are measureless.
Because of Love's rich legacy,
I vocalize exultantly.